G000115869

ABA Certification

David Mayer

2021-02-09

STUDY GUIDE

ABA Certification

Learn The Secrets To Quickly Pass The Aba Exams And Finally Get The Certifications That Enhance Yours Skills. Real Practice Test With Detailed Screenshots, Answers And Explanations

Index

How to Get a 50% Discount

If you have come this far and are curious about how to get a unique offer, then you surely understand it is essential for you to take the right ABA Certification now. There is no more time to waste; it's time to be certified in the right way according to your skills.

By purchasing this book you will then be entitled to an incredible 50% discount code on all products available at www.Certification-questions.com

It is a unique offer, and you will finally be able to understand which is the Certification required for your career, understand how to take the Exam and what are the prerequisites. Also, you will be able to use the only Simulated Exam that always has the latest questions available with 100% guaranteed success and a money back guarantee policy.

Don't wait, send us a copy to info@Certification-questions.com:

- of your book
- of your purchase receipt

And, we will automatically send you a discount code equal to 50% for the best Exam Simulator available on the market.

Thanks - Certification-questions.com

Introduction

Applied Behavior Analysis is a significantly preferred healing approach for stepping in when socially unacceptable actions start adversely influencing one's life. ABA therapy involves modifying and also reinforcing proper behaviors, from excellent health to social communication, to improve daily working. ABA was developed in the 1970s at the University of California-Los Angeles by scientists Ivan Lovaas and also Robert Koegel. Behavior analysts currently utilize ABA methods for several impairments, including autism, oppositional bold disorder, anxiety, bulimia, cerebral palsy, and manic depression, with wonderful success. Research from the Center for Evidence-Based Policy discovered that 92.9 percent of special demands youngsters treated with ABA presented positive progression. Supplying used applied behavior analysis solutions in 1:1 settings needs ending up being certified after ABA training.

This guide will cover all aspects of the ABA Exam Certifications. The author begins by discussing an intro to the ABA Certification exam in which he described the solid fundamental information of the concepts as well as a basic understanding of the certification exam which are following;

- Registration procedure of ABA certification exams
- Topics of ABA certification exams
- Benefits of ABA certification exams
- ABA certification exams requirements
- Certification path describes the knowledge of associated technologies and skills that are required to pass the ABA Certification Exam
- Duration of exam
- Exam format
- Available languages

- Certified professional salary in different countries
- Price of the ABA certification exams
- Difficulty in writing ABA certification exams
- Different solutions of ABA certification exams

This ABA Certification Study Guide covers 100% of exam information, ensuring that you have complete understanding to choose which is the right certification exam for you.

Copyright

PUBLISHED BY

certificaton-questions.com

Copyright @ 2019 Certification Questions

First Edition

This book is provided to expresses the author's views and opinions. The views and opinions expressed in this book including URLs and other Internet websites referenced may change without notice.

Any trademarks, service marks, product names or named features in this book are assumed to the property of their respective owners and are used only for reference. There is no implied endorsement if the author references one of these terms, logos, or trademarks.

Some examples given are provided for illustration and learning purposes, and are fictitious. No real association or connection is intended or inferred.

Dedication

Do you know how?

You choose a book then go to the Dedication Page and find that once again the author has dedicated a book to someone else and not to you.

Not this time.

This book is dedicated to the readers, as, without you, there would be no need for this book to have been written.

Hopefully the effort put into producing this resource guide will result in value and success when you sit your certification exam.

This one's for you. Thanks - Certification-questions.com

Acknowledgments

The world is better, thanks to people who want to develop and guide others. What makes it even better are the people who share the gift of their time to guide future leaders. Thank you to all who strive to grow and help others to grow.

Without the experience and support of my colleagues and team at Certification-questions.com, this book would not exist. You have given me the opportunity to lead a great group of people to become a leader of great leaders. It is a blessed place. Thanks to the Certification-questions.com team.

I want to say thank you to everyone who ever said anything positive to me or taught me something. It was your kind words and actions over the years that drove me to help others in my turn. THANK YOU.

PREFACE

Are you looking for valid Practice Tests for ABA Certification?

This book will guide on how you can pass the ABA Certification Exam using Practice Tests.

We will cover a large set of information for ABA Certification topics, so you will systemically discover how to pass the Certification exam.

This book will also explore many of your questions, such as:

- ABA Exam topics
- What are the essential criteria for passing the Official ABA Exam?
- How much ABA Exam Cost?
- What is the format of the ABA Exam?
- The advantage of ABA Exam Certification
- What are the difficulties of ABA Exam Certification?

We appreciate you taking the time to read this book, and we are really excited to assist you on your career growth journey.

How to Use This Book

There are four main components to the present ABA Study Guide.

First, the Introduction, in which you will get to know about the importance of ABA Certification and Practice Tests.

Secondly, the Table of Contents proves quite helpful for maneuvering through the ebook.

Thirdly, there is the Content, in which you will get to know about the different methods of studying for the ABA Certification Exam that will help you to pass the Certification Exam on your first attempt.

Fourthly, the Summary, in which you will read the brief statement or account of the main points of the ABA Certification Exam.

ABA Exams

ABA Certified Professionals form a unique community with ABA as its hub.Individuals can take advantage of the networking and professional growth opportunities which according to the research is a much more poignant aspect of the value of certification that was previously envisioned. ABA also recognizes that the community is an important way to engage with its customer base.

The **Certification-questions.com team** has worked directly with industry experts to provide you with the actual questions and answers from **the latest versions of the ABA exam**. Practice questions are proven to be the most effectively way of preparing for certification exams.

ABA certified professionals are certified individuals who specialize in ABA information technology programs and applications. Experts in the field of ABA programs, they focus their technical support skills in various areas, ranging from operating systems, cloud solutions to Web development.

With a certificate, your value increases when you apply for jobs. According to ABA your chances of getting **hired increases 5 times**. According to ABA, **86% of hiring managers indicate that they prefer job applicants having an IT certificate**. And ABA certification is a preference over some unknown computer training institutes' certificates. Eight out of ten Hiring Managers wish to verify the certificates provided by job applicants. Further, according to ABA, 64% of IT managers prefer ABA certificates to other certificates. Certification, training, and experience are the three main areas that provide better recognition to a person when it comes to promotions and incentives.

We offers an online service that allows students to study through tests questions. The Simulator is built to reflect the final exam structure: It is an excellent study material as it offers the ability to run an online actual exam. Every question is also associated with the solution and each solution is explained in detail.

Chapter 1: CRCM - Certified Regulatory Compliance Manager

Exam Guide

ABA Certified Regulatory Compliance Manager CRCM Exam:

ABA Certified Regulatory Compliance Manager CRCM Exam is related to Certified Regulatory Compliance Manager (CRCM) Professional Certification. This CRCM exam validates the Candidates knowledge and skills in wealth management and trust, compliance and risk management, lending, bank marketing and retirement services. Compliance Auditors and Compliance Officers usually holds or pursue this certification and you can expect the same job roles after completion of this certification.

CRCM Exam topics:

Candidates must know the exam topics before they start of preparation. Because it will really help them in hitting the core. Our **CRCM dumps** will include the following topics:

- Credit 35%
- Deposits 15%
- Bank Operations 15%
- Financial Crimes 20%
- CRA 5%
- Privacy 10%

Certification Path:

The Certified Regulatory Compliance Manager certification includes only one CRCM exam.

Who should take the CRCM exam:

The ABA Certified Regulatory Compliance Manager CRCM Exam certification is an internationally-recognized validation that identifies persons who earn it as possessing skilled as an Certified Regulatory Compliance Manager. If a candidate wants significant improvement in career growth needs enhanced knowledge, skills, and talents. The ABA Certified Regulatory Compliance Manager CRCM Exam certification provides proof of this advanced knowledge and skill. If a candidate has knowledge of associated technologies and skills that are required to pass ABA Certified Regulatory Compliance Manager CRCM Exam then he should take this exam.

How to study the CRCM Exam:

There are two main types of resources for preparation of certification exams first there are the study guides and the books that are detailed and suitable for building knowledge from ground up then there are video tutorial and lectures that can somehow ease the pain of through study and are comparatively less boring for some candidates yet these demand time and concentration from the learner. Smart Candidates who want to build a solid foundation in all exam topics and related technologies usually combine video lectures with study guides to reap the benefits of both but there is one crucial preparation tool as often overlooked by most candidates the practice exams. Practice exams are built to make students comfortable with the real exam environment. Statistics have shown that most students fail not due to that preparation but due to exam anxiety the fear of the unknown. Certification-questions.com expert team recommends you to prepare some notes on these topics along with it don't forget to practice CRCM Exam dumps which been written by our expert team, Both these will help you a lot to clear this exam with good marks.

How much CRCM Exam Cost:

The price of the CRCM exam is $750 USD.

How to book the CRCM Exam:

These are following steps for registering the CRCM exam.
Step 1: Check the eligibility requirements to determine if you qualify.
Step 2: Review the exam dates below.
Step 3: Purchase the exam. Payment must be made by credit card.
(You will be prompted to create a Certification Manager account.)
Step4: Complete and submit the application

What is the duration of the CRCM Exam:

- Format: Multiple choices, multiple answers
- Length of Examination: 4 hours
- Number of Questions: 200

     The benefit in Obtaining the CRCM Exam Certification:

- Certified Regulatory Compliance Manager differentiate yourself with a credential that sets the standard of professional expertise in the compliance field.
- Certified Regulatory Compliance Manager receive a free electronic subscription to ABA Bank Compliance magazine
- Certified Regulatory Compliance Manager can get relevant professional development options quickly and easily with the Certification Manager, which highlights programs that have been approved for CE credit.
- Certified Regulatory Compliance Manager receive special pricing for registration to the following conferences:
  ABA/ABA Financial Crimes Enforcement Conference
  ABA Regulatory Compliance Conference

ABA Risk Management Conference

Difficulty in writing CRCM Exam:

Mostly job holder candidates give a short time to their study and want to pass the exam with good marks. Thereby we have many ways to prepare and practice for exams in a very short time that help the candidates to ready for exams in a very short time without any tension. Candidates can easily prepare CRCM exams from Certification-questions because we are providing the best **CRCM exam dumps** which are verified by our experts. Certification-questions has always verified and updated **CRCM dumps** that helps the candidate to prepare his exam with little effort in a very short time. We also provide latest and relevant study guide material which is very useful for a candidate to prepare easily for **CRCM exam dumps**. Candidate can download and read the latest dumps in PDF and VCE format. Certification-questions is providing real questions of **CRCM dumps**. We are very fully aware of the importance of student time and money that's why Certification-questions give the candidate the most astounding brain dumps having all the inquiries answer outlined and verified by our experts.

For more info visit::

ABA CRCM Exam Reference

Sample Practice Test for CRCM

Question: 1 *One Answer Is Right*

To be effective, compliance risk management professionals must design a framework to ensure that bank management understands the risks and the steps that must be taken to mitigate them. The many roles compliance professionals fill incorporate risk management aspects including:

Answers:

A) Coordinating regulatory exams to explain risks to examiners

B) Overseeing compliance training targeting higher risk areas

C) Tracking regulatory proposals and final rules to understand new risks

D) All of these

Solution: D

Question: 2 *One Answer Is Right*

They also embrace the concept of risk-based compliance management. They expect compliance management to be tailored to the bank, be it large or small, offering standard or specialty financial services, simple or complex products lines, and adjusted as appropriate for the customer base as that issued for the Bank Secrecy Act, also establishes their expectations that a bank's program be risk based. Who are they?

Answers:

A) Outsourcing firms

B) Foreign financial service providers

C) Bank regulatory agencies

D) Risk management organizations

Solution: C

Question: 3 *One Answer Is Right*

A compliance professional's responsibilities include all of the following EXCEPT:

Answers:

A) Understanding the business units operating environment and risk tolerance

B) Performing risk assessments with the assistance of business units to determine current risk levels and risks associated with the bank's products, lines of business, customers, and locations, among other factors

C) Working with business units to ensure prompt corrective action for any detected errors

D) Assisting business lines with compliance training for employees, as needed

Solution: D

Question: 4 *One Answer Is Right*

_____ should include basic elements designed to understand and mitigate risk. It usually includes: Written program Compliance-related policies and procedures

Answers:

A) Tactical Compliance procedure

B) Rank solution

C) Compliance program

D) None of these

Solution: C

Question: 5 *One Answer Is Right*

In a compliance program, tactical compliance procedures should be integrated into business line procedures, such as how to deliver an Adverse Action Notice when an application is declined. In this case:

Answers:

A) Regulations should be applied consistently to procedures throughout the bank

B) Revisions to procedures should be based on compliance expertise and not mere editing

C) Providing solutions to mitigate any identified risk

D) Assisting business units in developing or revising policies and procedures to reflect current regulatory requirements

Solution: A, B

Question: 6 *One Answer Is Right*

Which of the following should be done during research and interpreting regulations Compliance professionals in mitigating compliance risk?

Answers:

A) Track regulatory proposals

B) Implementing final regulatory rules

C) Understanding the business units' operating environment and risk tolerance

D) Ranking solutions as high, moderate and low risk

Solution: A, B, D

Question: 7 *One Answer Is Right*

The compliance program should address plans to verify adherence to applicable regulations through:

Answers:

A) Ongoing monitoring to evaluate the program, self monitoring and corrective action

B) Self monitoring

C) Periodic reviews

D) Ongoing monitoring to evaluate the program, self monitoring and periodic reviews

Solution: A

Question: 8 *One Answer Is Right*

There is no established template for documenting compliance risk. Each institution should develop a risk assessment that fits its risk profile. The components that are commonly used throughout the industry are as follows EXCEPT:

Answers:

A) Risk assessment

B) Measuring key risk indicators

C) Identifying key performance indicators

D) Training the leadership of compliance regulation program

Solution: D

Question: 9 *One Answer Is Right*

In Compliance regulation and risk assessment key performance indicators usually include:

Answers:

A) Fines or penalties

B) Customer complaints

C) Regulatory criticism from a regulator or internal or external auditors

D) None of these

Solution: A, B, C

Question: 10 *One Answer Is Right*

For example on a 0-5 scale:

A simple risk map based on this example might look like the following

	Exposure Low	Exposure Moderate	Exposure High
Likelihood High	Mod – 2	High – 4	High – 5
Likelihood Moderate	Low – 1	Mod – 3	High – 4
Likelihood Low	Low – 0	Mod – 2	Mod – 3

The risk trend shows the direction of risk and probable change to risk over the next 12 months. A trend toward increasing risk means that

Answers:

A) Management may want to take additional action through more controls or increased reviews

B) Risk may prompt a decrease in controls and improved efficiencies

C) Controls currently in place are appropriate to succeed in keeping risks within management's established risk-tolerance level

D) Risk measurements exceed management's tolerance for risk

Solution: A

Chapter 2: CTFA - Certified Trust and Financial Advisor

Exam Guide

ABA Certified Trust and Financial Advisor CTFA Exam:

ABA Certified Trust and Financial Advisor CTFA Exam is related to Certified Trust and Financial Advisor Professional Certification. This CRCM exam validates the Candidates knowledge and skills in fiduciary and trust activities, financial planning, tax law and planning and investment management. Bankers, Brokers, Financial Planners, Tax and Trust Professionals usually holds or pursue this certification and you can expect the same job roles after completion of this certification.

CTFA Exam topics:

Candidates must know the exam topics before they start of preparation. Because it will really help them in hitting the core. Our **CTFA dumps** will include the following topics:

*   Fiduciary & Trust Activities 25%
*   Financial Planning 25%
*   Tax Law & Planning 25%
*   Investment Management 20%
*   Ethics 5%

    Certification Path:

The Certified Trust and Financial Advisor certification includes only one CTFA exam.

Who should take the CTFA exam:

The ABA Certified Trust and Financial Advisor CTFA Exam certification is an internationally-recognized validation that identifies persons who earn it as possessing skilled as an Certified Trust and Financial Advisor. If a candidate wants significant improvement in career growth needs enhanced knowledge, skills, and talents. The ABA Certified Trust and Financial Advisor CTFA Exam certification provides proof of this advanced knowledge and skill. If a candidate has knowledge and skills that are required to pass ABA Certified Trust and Financial Advisor CTFA Exam then he should take this exam.

How to study the CTFA Exam:

There are two main types of resources for preparation of certification exams first there are the study guides and the books that are detailed and suitable for building knowledge from ground up then there are video tutorial and lectures that can somehow ease the pain of through study and are comparatively less boring for some candidates yet these demand time and concentration from the learner. Smart Candidates who want to build a solid foundation in all exam topics and related technologies usually combine video lectures with study guides to reap the benefits of both but there is one crucial preparation tool as often overlooked by most candidates the practice exams. Practice exams are built to make students comfortable with the real exam environment. Statistics have shown that most students fail not due to that preparation but due to exam anxiety the fear of the unknown. Certification-questions.com expert team recommends you to prepare some notes on these topics along with it don't forget to practice CTFA Exam dumps which been written by our expert team, Both these will help you a lot to clear this exam with good marks.

How much CTFA Exam Cost:

The price of the CTFA exam is $750 USD.

How to book the CTFA Exam:

These are following steps for registering the CTFA exam.
Step 1: Check the eligibility requirements to determine if you qualify.
Step 2: Review the exam dates below.
Step 3: Purchase the exam. Payment must be made by credit card.
(You will be prompted to create a Certification Manager account.)
Step4: Complete and submit the application

What is the duration of the CTFA Exam:

- Format: Multiple choices, multiple answers
- Length of Examination: 4 hours
- Number of Questions: 200

  The benefit in Obtaining the CTFA Exam Certification:

- Gain Employer Recognition for promotions and raises
- Score ABA job opportunities
- Capture the attention of recruiters
- This CTFA exam covers a different technology to meet the needs of varying job roles

  Difficulty in writing CTFA Exam:

This exam is very difficult especially for those who have not on the job experience as an ABA Certified Trust and Financial Advisor. Candidates can not pass this exam with only taking courses because courses do not provide the knowledge and skills that are necessary to pass this exam. Certification-questions.com is the best platform for those who want to pass CTFA with good grades in no time. Certification-questions.com provides the latest CTFA exam dumps that will immensely help candidates to get good grades in their final

CTFA exam. Certification-questions.com is one of the best study sources to provide the most updated **CTFA Exam Dumps** with our CTFA Exam Questions PDF. Candidate can rest guaranteed that they will pass their CTFA Exam on the first attempt. We will also save candidates valuable time. Certification-questions Dumps help to pass the exam easily. Candidates can get all real questions from Certification-questions. One of the best parts is we also provide most updated CTFA Exam study materials and we also want a candidate to be able to access study materials easily whenever they want. So, We provide all our CTFA exam questions in a very common PDF format that is accessible from all devices.

For more info visit::

ABA CTFA Exam Reference

Sample Practice Test for CTFA

Question: 1 *One Answer Is Right*

Financial goals cove a wide range of financial aspirations such as:

Answers:

A) Controlling living expenses

B) Meeting retirement needs

C) Setting up a savings and investment program

D) All of the above

Solution: D

Question: 2 *One Answer Is Right*

These are target dates in the future when certain financial objectives are expected to be completed. What are these?

Answers:

A) Goal dates

B) Target dates

C) Due dates

D) Financial dates

Solution: A

Question: 3 *One Answer Is Right*

Today's well-defined employee benefits package cover a full spectrum of benefits that may include all EXCEPT:

Answers:

A) Long -term care insurance

B) Dental and vision care

C) Subsidized employee benefit plan

D) Partial retirement plans

Solution: D

Question: 4 *One Answer Is Right*

Tax deferred retirement plans and flexible spending accounts offer tax advantages. Some retirement plans allow you to_____ against them.

Answers:

A) Lend

B) Borrow

C) Spend

D) None of the above

Solution: B

Question: 5 *One Answer Is Right*

Accumulating assets to enjoy in retirement is only part of the:

Answers:

A) Long-term financial planning process

B) Short-term financial planning process

C) Life time financial planning process

D) Permanent financial planning process

Solution: A

Question: 6 *One Answer Is Right*

This is a type of employee benefit plan wherein the employer allocates a certain amount of money and then the employee spends that money for benefits selected from a menu covering everything from child care to health and life insurance to retirement benefits.

Answers:

A) Flexible benefit plan

B) Cafeteria plan

C) Short-term financial plan

D) Both of the above are one and the same

Solution: D

Question: 7 *One Answer Is Right*

Most financial planners fall into one of two categories based on how they are paid. Commission based planners earn commissions on the financial products they sell, whereas _____ charge fees based on the complexity of the plan they prepare.

Answers:

A) Free only planners

B) Commission based planners

C) Professional planners

D) Security planners

Solution: A

Question: 8 *One Answer Is Right*

When determining the interaction between the UK and EU on the regulation of the financial services industry, the UK government must always

Answers:

A) seek approval from the European Commission before implementing any new regulations.

B) implement new EU Directives by passing acts of Parliament.

C) accommodate all EU Decisions in UK legislation.

D) provide copies of new regulation to the European Commission within a reasonable period of time for their approval.

Solution: B

Question: 9 *One Answer Is Right*

A client has previously written to her former adviser opting out of any marketing activities from the firm or any third parties. However she continues to receive direct investment offers from the firm. She should complain based on the firm not complying with which set of regulations?

Answers:

A) Conduct of Business rules.

B) Data Protection Act 1998.

C) Distance Selling Regulations.

D) Treating Customers Fairly.

Solution: B

Question: 10 *One Answer Is Right*

The Financial Services and Markets Act 2000 regulates the provision of which type(s) of financial advice?

Answers:

A) Advice to vulnerable individuals only

B) Advice to all individuals

C) Advice to all individuals and group personal pensions schemes only

D) Advice to all individuals unless they are elective professional clients

Solution: B

SUMMARY

To recap, main stages of certification exam study guide are Introduction to ABA Exam , ABA Exam topics in which Candidates must know the exam topics before they start of preparation, ABA Exam Requirements, Cost of ABA Exam, registration procedure of the ABA Exam, ABA Exam formate, ABA Exam Certified salary, ABAExam advantages.

If you are aspirant to pass the cerification exam, start exam preparation with study material provided by Certification-questions.com

About The Author

<u>David Mayer</u>

Co-Founder of Certification-Questions.com

David is the Co-founder of Certification-Questions.com, one of the largest Certification practice tests and PDF exams websites on the Internet. They are providing dumps an innovative way by providing Online Web Simulator and Mobile App. He likes to share his knowledge and is active in the ABA community.

He has written several books, blogs, and is active in the ABA community.

APPENDIX

Certification

The action or process of providing someone or something with an official document that accredits a state or level of results.

Practice test

The practical exam is an alternative, non-scoring version of the intermediate or final exam of the course. The practice exam has the same format as the "real" exam, which means that if the practice exam has 20 multiple-choice questions and four free-answer questions, the "real" exam will be the same.